30 Days to Better Self-Care

Building Your Intentional Life One Step at a Time

Sonya L. Sigler

Your Intentional Life Series

30 Days to Better Self-Care: Building Your Intentional Life One Step at a Time is a work of my own creation.

PractiGal is a trademark of Sonya L Sigler. www.sonyasigler.com

The ideas and encouragements expressed in this journal do not replace the advice of a medical professional or trained therapist. Consult your physician before making any changes to your diet or regular health plan.

The information in this book was correct at the time of publication, and the Author does not assume any liability for loss or damage caused by errors or omissions, again, this is my perspective, opinion, and experience, so it has been written as such.

ISBN - 978-1-961185-48-7 paperback

Cover photo courtesy of Vero Manrique

www.inomniaparatuspublishing.com

This workbook is dedicated to all the women who are overwhelmed on a daily basis with everything life throws at them and want a different path forward!

There are several opportunities throughout this workbook to take a pause and color

Building Your Intentional Life

Your Intentional Life is a series of workbooks aimed at helping you build your intentional life one step at a time.

It took me a long time to learn how to build an intentional life. I must confess that I spent many years following the path of 'should'... You should go to college, you should get married, you should have 2.5 children... those societal messages were loud and over-shadowed my own voice.

All these 'should' activities came to a head when I ended up in the emergency room thinking I was having a heart attack two days before I turned 35. Spoiler alert – I didn't have a heart attack! What I did have was a severely out of whack over-active thyroid which forced me to make some significant changes in my life.

Now, I don't want you to experience such a drastic health crisis to make changes in your life. What I learned was simple in theory and much harder in practice. 1) Be intentional about taking care of myself and what is important to me; and 2) Stay in alignment with those priorities, wants, and needs.

Be Intentional

First, I had to get off autopilot and become thoughtful and considerate about what I wanted or needed. Since my body was the impetuous to make changes, I began there. I started small, paying attention to exercise routines before moving on to my eating habits. Sticking to observing, evaluating, and changing one aspect at a time was my key to long-term success.

Stay in Alignment
Second, I had to stay in alignment with my priorities. Learning to say no was a big part of this change. If I was asked to do something that wasn't in alignment with my goals and priorities, I politely declined, learned to say no, AND to be OK with that. My old people-pleasing, good girl habits died a hard death. In short, I had to learn to set and keep boundaries, and to be accountable to myself.

The earned confidence from putting a boundary in place and keeping it is invaluable. The clarity resulting from staying in alignment with what I wanted was freeing. The result has been a sanctuary - a life filled, once again, with love and laughter. It's a much happier, healthier life I don't need a vacation from.

As you begin your own journey to build your intentional life, starting with this 30 days' focus on self-care, take a moment to appreciate yourself for taking this step forward. Remember to...

Be Intentional

Stay in Alignment

Making the Most of this Workbook

30 Days to Better Self-Care

This book is not your usual self-care advice or typical 30-day challenge which may tell you to go outside for 15 minutes or try a new recipe or take a 24-hour break from social media.

These 30 Days are laid out as four weeks of self-care topics to observe, assess, and change your self-care (only if you determine a change is needed), plus a beginning and ending assessment to see where you are.

To get the most out of this workbook you'll want to peruse the overview of the 30 Days' topics. Each Day prompt is an opportunity to pay attention to a particular aspect of your self-care (or in my case when I first started this self-care journey, the lack of self-care). Taking the time to observe what is or isn't happening will inform you if a change is needed.

The cycle I recommend following is:
- Meditation/Observation/Reflection – take a moment to notice what 'is' for you
- Writing/Notate – there is ample space to document your observations for each Day
- Make a Change/Learn/Grow – make a change if you want and then reevaluate

Although the information on self-care is laid out as 30 days, your use of this workbook doesn't have to be sequential, feel free to pick it up, or put it down as needed given everything else you have going on in your life.

Self-care can be done in any amount of time you have whether it's five minutes (neck and shoulder rolls) or five hours (visit a museum) because it's not really about the amount of time or a particular activity. It is about your intention and action.

Where your attention goes, energy flows.

As you assess what self-care means to you and evaluate what you are doing to take care of yourself, you can adjust or make changes as needed or desired. Though I make suggestions here or share examples of what works and what doesn't for me, the changes you choose to make for yourself are up to you.

You can use this workbook anytime you feel overwhelmed or stuck in your life. Think of this as an opportunity to take a closer look at what self-care looks like for you, your health, and your intentional life.

If you'd like to share your progress or seek advice, you can post your observations in the PractiGal Career Mentor Facebook Group https://www.facebook.com/groups/practigal

Who am I?

If you haven't met me yet, my name is Sonya Sigler.

I've been an IP and corporate lawyer for over 30 years, starting at SEGA (that's me with Tom Kalinske, the SEGA CEO when I worked there) and Intuit before leaving the law behind (or so I thought).

Lawyer

I've been an entrepreneur since 2000, working in start-ups in the AI, Legal, and Gaming industries as an executive in the legal, finance, operations, business development and marketing functions. I am not afraid to take on those big crazy, hairy projects that no one else wants to touch. I call it organizing chaos. I've built a contracts management database at practically every place I've worked.

Entrepreneur

I've been speaking to audiences all over the world since giving training in copyrights, trademarks, and patents at Intuit. I speak on self-care along with a variety of other topics including AI competence and confidence, grant writing, empowering women, and authentic personal branding. I am a certified Vistage speaker.

Speaker

Community Theater

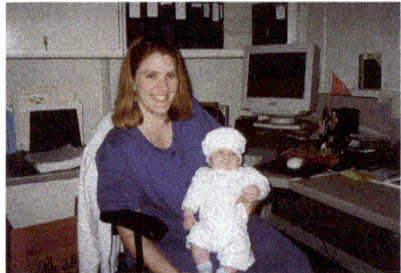

Advocate for Women

Philanthropist

Autocrossing Porsches

From the pictures, you're probably thinking, 'this lady is crazy'... that may be, but, as you can see, I have many roles and interests and I do a lot of things because I am a lifelong learner with an insatiable intellectual curiosity. I also have ADHD which leads me to become interested in something for five minutes (making sourdough bread) or five decades (music)!

My journey into self-care or, as I like to think about it, boundary setting and keeping, has been a journey not unlike the paths highlighted in those old Family Circus cartoons. I'll share stories about this transformation from burnout and overwhelm to living a life I don't need a vacation from.

I try to integrate my work and personal life, to see friends and family when I travel for work. I have many hobbies including singing, dancing, and acting in community theater. I've played trombone since I was 10 and recently joined a choir. I am a philanthropist and teach others grant writing.

A few years ago, I realized two things:
- If you don't care for yourself, who will?
- What do I want to do to take care of me and the one body I have?

Answering these two questions led me to lead a more intentional life and make drastic changes (divorce and job change at the same time, which I do NOT recommend), and more subtle changes (like eliminating processed foods and eating good, whole foods and keeping my kitchen clean).

Now I help others make this same kind of transformation in their personal and professional lives

My three boys

My forever husband

Let's Connect

As an author, speaker, coach and consultant, I offer a wide variety of books, workbooks, on-demand courses, workshops, and other services. For more information, please connect with me!

**My linktree has all my current resources:
https://linktr.ee/ssigler**

Importance of Self-care

You never know what is going in with someone.

She (Cheslie Kryst, former Miss USA, and correspondent for 'Extra') seemingly had it all - beauty, brains, and an amazing job related to solving social justice causes she cared deeply about. And given the outcome (dead at 30), I'm guessing she also had the accompanying stress, pressure, depression, and anxiety, which run high in the legal industry.

Mental health issues and self-care aren't issues that are going away anytime soon. Self-care isn't merely a day at the spa.

Self-care is the *process* of figuring out how you thrive and doing those things to support you and your good mental health - whether it's exercising to work off the stress or work through issues that are causing you anxiety or maybe it is building a support network of people you can call when things become too overwhelming or you start to feel like it is all too much.

Use this workbook to develop your own self-care plan, using what works for you and discarding what doesn't.

You are worth it.

30 Days Overview

Day 1.   Assessment
Day 2.   Morning Routine
Day 3.   Eating/Drinking Habits
Day 4.   Evening Routine
Day 5.   Mental Health
Day 6.   Exercise Routine
Day 7.   *Week 1 Observations*
Day 8.   (Re)define Self-care
Day 9.   Energizing
Day 10.   Depleting
Day 11.   Reframing Beliefs
Day 12.   Intentions
Day 13.   Letting Go
Day 14.   *Week 2 Observations*
Day 15.   Making Changes
Day 16.   Lifestyle
Day 17.   Work Style
Day 18.   Family Time
Day 19.   Resetting
Day 20.   Finances
Day 21.   *Week 3 Observations*
Day 22.   Self-care Toolbox
Day 23.   Priorities
Day 24.   Retooled Routines
Day 25.   Saying No
Day 26.   Taking Risks
Day 27.   Support System
Day 28.   *Week 4 Observations*
Day 29.   Takeaways
Day 30.   Celebrate

A Few Quick Tips

To get the most out of your efforts, I recommend the following cycle for each day:

- **Review the Day's prompt**
- **Meditate/Observe/Reflect** – take a moment to notice what 'is' for you
- **Write About It** – there is ample space to document your observations for each Day
- **Make a Change/Learn/Grow** – make a change if you want and then reevaluate whether it helps

There is a bullet journal page at the end of each Day to make a list of things you want to do or change.

Sprinkled throughout, you'll also find a few images to color if you need to take a break.

If you need more support, I've recorded a few meditations you might find helpful.

Day 1 - Assessment

How are you doing? What are you doing to take care of yourself now?

You'll spend the first seven days observing and evaluating what you are doing for self-care. Think of it as an audit or assessment of sorts, where you evaluate what you are doing/not doing. Or use a rating scale, a grade, or whatever you choose - it's just for you and your information.

A few years ago, when I looked at my life and how I was taking care of myself, I became very specific about what self-care means to me:
- Eat good healthy, whole foods
- Exercise everyday (walking is great, running is better)
- Take time to connect with family and others on a daily basis
- Take time for writing and meditation
- Automate everything money-wise
- Take time to do what I love – I have MANY hobbies
- Take time to connect with family on a daily basis

This list is what made sense for me. The great thing about self-care is that you get to define what it means to you and put your own list together over the next 30 days.

What does self-care mean to you?

Give yourself
permission to pause.

Day 2 - Morning Routine

Today, look at your morning routines.

Some people drink coffee or tea and sit for a few quiet minutes before waking others or making breakfast or checking their phone or email.

Currently, I have a very flaky morning routine – it's never the same thing twice because it depends on what's scheduled that day and when my day starts with obligations involving others.

Usually, I begin with a gratitude practice as I open my eyes, naming three things I am grateful for. I may write these down later in my journal, but even that had been hit or miss lately.

Sometimes, I get dressed and head outside to exercise, but frequently, I find myself looking at email, texts/Line/WhatsApp, or play word games. If I have client calls or a presentation, then I will make myself presentable and start with those. And somewhere in there I will feed the cats.

My morning routine varies so much. I think I preferred when we lived in California and I exercised furst thing, to enjoy the sunshine and then my chai tea latte at Starbucks, before starting my day.

What do you include in your morning routine to set your day up for success, or put your best foot forward? What, if anything, do you do to nurture yourself?

The morning is what you make it.

Day 3 - Eating/Drinking Habits

Today's self-care topic is eating/drinking habits (water, coffee/tea, soda, alcohol, etc.).

Look at your eating/drinking habits and routines - this is for assessment purposes not for judgment.

One thing I've noticed lately is that I need to get back to eating a healthy, protein rich breakfast. I've gotten into a habit of not eating in the morning and then wondering why I can't think straight.

Or I eat something to begin with and then work until 2 pm without moving and then wonder why I'm hungry/tired. Thankfully, what I do eat is healthy and I need to stay vigilant to avoid sugar/sweets.

Unfortunately, I've also noticed if I drink red wine, it keeps me awake or gives me night sweats. Neither of which do I want. So, I've severely limited the red wine drinking. And moved on to cocktails, tea, or hot water with lemon.

What's working/not working for your eating/hydration habits?

You are what you eat.
Is it true?

Day 4 - Evening Routine

What do you do to wind down in the evening and get good sleep?

I was most successful with an evening routine when my boys were at their dad's house for the week, and I was by myself. The 10 pm alarm would signal bedtime and I would prepare for bed then read 6 pages of a dense book before going to sleep, and thankfully staying asleep until 6 am.

Now that I'm remarried and my kids are (mostly) out of the house, it doesn't quite work as well. Sometimes we stay up late binge watching something. Sometimes I go to bed at 10 or 11 pm and my hubby stays up late, usually waking me (the light sleeper) when he comes to bed.

It's best when I stick to a consistent wind down routine. And I must say, reading a physical book still puts me to sleep after a few pages.

How is your bedtime routine? Is it consistent? Does it work?

Is there anything preventing you from sleeping well?

"Sleep is the best meditation."
Dalai Lama

Day 5 - Mental Health

How is your mental health routine? What do you do to take a break, get back on track, or reset mentally?

Mostly I start with removing myself from the situation I'm in - getting up and walking around, going to the bathroom, leaving the room, etc.

I made a list of things that help me reset and get back on track - knitting, reading, a walk, journaling. Meditation is on that list but occasionally I am so out of sorts it doesn't help.

Over time I have learned to watch out for two things: 1) when I am so overwhelmed I start flaking on things I want to do, and 2) when I start to have suicidal thoughts. At that point, I must do two things. First, I need to exercise outside, preferably in the sunshine. And second, I need to take a hard look at what I can control in my schedule and stop all other things that are not required.

Fundamentally, I withdraw from everything to take a self-imposed mental health/rest day doing errands, an outdoor activity or visiting a friend or my mom. Basically, anything but being in front of a computer.

Do you recognize when you need a break?

What do you do to reset mentally?

Sometimes you just need a break.

Day 6 - Exercise Routine

Today's topic is your exercise routine... if you have one.

How does your body feel? What clues does your body give you that you need to pay more attention to?

Having a Thai massage two days in a row made it apparent how much stress I've been holding in my feet, hips, and shoulders. I feel like all I've done is identify areas on my body that need attention.

Daily exercise routines have gone to hell since we moved to Washington (right before the Pandemic) and it rains so much here that my exercise regimen's become extremely flaky - maybe I take a walk, maybe a run, maybe a bike ride. Mostly walking or nothing.

My hubby and I will do a yoga routine on Netflix, which is relaxing before bedtime. But, I find myself wanting to do yoga in a studio for the camaraderie and go to a gym with boot camp for the competition and being told what to do (I don't want to have to think up an exercise to do).

What's working/not working for you and exercise?

Something is better than nothing.

Day 7 - Week 1 Observations

Ok - you've spent this first week taking an audit or assessing your efforts to understand your needs and take care of yourself.

You looked at your morning and evening routines, your eating/drinking habits, and how you're taking care of your body, your mental health, and your exercise routines.

Looking back over what transpired, my first observation is that I need to put some better routines in place for almost everything. They've gotten out of whack to the point where they need an overhaul! Mostly around exercise.

Being in uncontrolled situations, like walking in a crowd where people can bump into me, saps my energy, and make me extremely tired.

How did you fare in your assessment?

What observations do you have? Do you need to make any changes?

If so, what small changes can you make this coming week that feel helpful and won't be overwhelming?

Overhaul, changes, or minor tweaks?

Day 8 - (Re)define Self-care

What does self-care mean to you? Do you need to shift your mindset around what self-care is?

My mindset has evolved over the last 10 years, and I've developed a list of what I can do to take good care of myself. I keep that list in the front of my notebook.

Before shifting my thinking around self-care, I would have considered attending yoga class or going to get a pedicure as self-care. I still do think of those as self-care but more like a moment in time rather than a strategy or way of thinking.

Keeping a clean and clear kitchen has been one of the most surprising self-care tools for me. I like waking up to a clean kitchen rather than a mess. I find that it is easier to spend a few minutes cleaning up at the end of the day to enjoy the clean kitchen when I come downstairs in the morning. It's calming for me.

How can you think differently about your self-care and what it means to you?

Where/how would you like to shift your thinking?

Self-care is the process of figuring out how *you* thrive.

_____

_____

_____

_____

_____

_____

_____

_____

_____

_____

_____

_____

_____

_____

_____

_____

_____

_____

_____

Day 9 - Energizing

What is energizing, inspiring, or resetting for you?

Hosting gatherings is energizing for me. It's been nice to do more hosting the last year. It's one of the things I missed most during the pandemic isolation. Brainstorming and generating ideas is energizing for me. Planning travel is energizing for me. Inspiring others is energizing for me - I love doing these things.

What's also working for me is time with my family. I spent two weeks in Thailand with my brother and his family when my nieces were on Spring Break. I spent it unplugged, being present, hanging out with my nieces, exploring astronomy, and the world around us.

Even though I did very little writing and knitting, it was all good. I was there for them, as my younger nieces are at the stage where they ask about 30 questions a minute, which was fun.

My point is figure out what energizes you and keeps your mental health at an equilibrium or on the positive side and do more of that.

What are you doing that energizes you and fills your tank? How can you work more of that into your life?

Make a list for yourself and try to do more of these things.

Look within.

Day 10 - Depleting

What saps your energy?

The top of my list is to minimize any time spent with negative people. I have this mental attitude if you don't like how something is, change it. That includes who you are spending your time with.

Commuting in traffic is an energy zapper for me. Listening to an audio book or podcast or calling friends and family during that time minimizes the traffic irritation.

Also, I noticed new activities, like walking through Chinatown in Bangkok, sap all my energy - too many noises, too many people (touching me, bumping into me), too many things to look at... it's all overwhelming. After this activity, I noticed I required quiet and stillness to recover, and maybe a hot cup of tea too.

Make a list of all those energy suckers. Try to eliminate, avoid, or minimize these activities.

Meet your expectations,
not other's expectations for you

Day 11 - Reframing Beliefs

What does it really mean to care for yourself? Time alone? Skincare? Staying true to yourself? Learning to ask for help?

For me, one of my self-care game changers has been learning to ask for help.

Five years ago, I wouldn't have thought to put 'learning to ask for help' into my self-care toolbox, but it is one of the most useful tools I have. I've embraced the belief that I don't have to do it all or do it alone.

Building my partnership with my husband is what led me to actually see the value of asking for help, not just providing help to others.

A second game changer for me was deciding to keep my kitchen clean each night before going to bed. It was so demoralizing waking up and coming out to dirty dishes in the kitchen, so spending 10-15 minutes cleaning before heading to bed became an act of self-care for me. Reframing the belief of 'I have to clean the kitchen' to one of taking care of myself has changed my whole attitude towards cleaning the kitchen.

How can you reframe self-care for yourself?

Which beliefs no longer serve you?

Day 12 - Intentions

What's next to incorporate into your life and routines? Being intentional can make such a difference in your level of satisfaction with your life. What changes do you *want* to make?

Staying off autopilot and being intentional about my daily actions helps keep me focused and grounded. When I find myself overwhelmed, it's usually because I have reverted back to autopilot mode.

I want/need to get into a better fitness routine/pattern/mindset! I slept better with regular exercise, and better sleep has moved to the top of my self-care list.

Meal planning is the other area I have to be vigilant and intentional about, otherwise, without a plan, I find myself reaching for carbs and sugar heavy foods.

Are you operating on autopilot?

Where can you be more intentional in your life?

Good intentions
require good action.

Day 13 - Letting Go

What can you let go of? Expectations, groups, obligations, people, habits?

When I was on that unplugged vacation to Thailand, I let go of almost all obligations that week. I had one client call which I chose not to reschedule even though it meant getting up at 2:30 am while on vacation. I figured, it's one day, not a big deal.

Argh! I screwed up the time by an hour and missed it which meant I had to reschedule anyway. Boo. Usually, I would have dwelled on it and beat myself up, but now I realize that's a waste of time and energy. I've learned that letting go of beliefs/actions that no longer serve me is a skill I need to hone.

What is no longer serving you?

What do you need/want to let go of?

Letting go is
easier than you think.

Day 14 - Week 2 Observations

What are your observations from the second week of focusing on your self-care?

Well, I guess my biggest observation is that I need to take a vacation and unplug more often. I love vacations (who doesn't) but it was the complete unplugging that made the difference. It was refreshing.

We enjoyed so much laughter, which was invigorating. I tried so many new things - like petting a tiger, feeding an elephant, eating bee larva, and eating pig's blood. New stuff makes life a memorable adventure!

My favorite part was hanging out with my nieces because I won't get this time back with them. Unplugging has been good, and I want to incorporate more of that into my life.

Did you notice any trends or patterns?

Did you experience any mind shifts or reframes around your self-care?

Rethinking requires reflection time.

Helpful Self-care Resources

If you are looking for other ideas about self-care and what it can look like for you, I have gathered a few helpful resources.

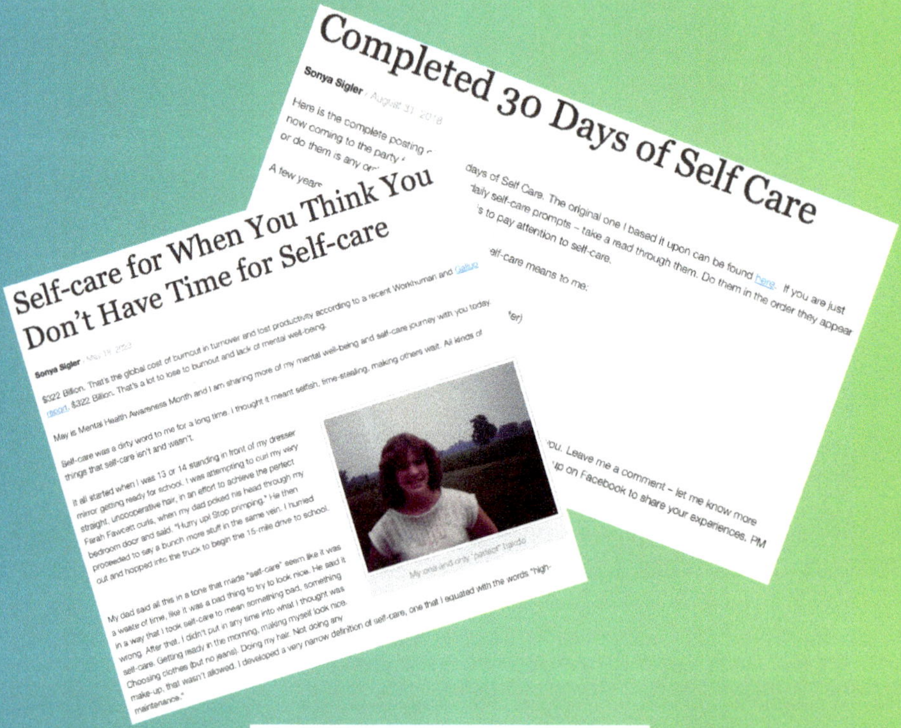

Day 15 - Making Changes

Do you need to make some changes around your self-care?

After having traveled for three weeks and eaten all kinds of different foods (not all of them good for me), I noticed a need to meal plan. Planning out our meals for the week and having egg cups or other protein-based food ready for breakfast is better for my body and mind.

One of the other things that I've been thinking about is finding a regular yoga class or boot camp. As much as I like walking/running around our neighborhood, I find that I like the group aspect of classes and I like being told what to do and not having to think. In the meantime, I need to up my vitamin D intake without any sunshine.

What changes are you thinking about making, or have you made already?

What do you hope the outcome of such changes will be?

Changes are inevitable.

Day 16 - Lifestyle

Does your lifestyle bring out the best in you?

For years we had soccer on Saturday and football and soccer on Sunday for my three boys and their seven teams. What that meant was go go go and not much quiet time. Our lifestyle then didn't have a ton of restorative time built in. We had to use the nooks and crannies of time to read, do nothing, makes cookies, etc.

Once the boys started high school, we got our weekends back and that allowed me to incorporate gardening and reading for fun back into my life.

Another time that sticks out in my mind is when we were on vacation in Florida. We were standing in the classic snaky Disneyworld line with what felt like everyone else and their brother when the ride broke down and closed. With everyone being tired and cranky, we decided to leave the park and go back to the hotel.

The kids could have cared less about Disney and the rides. They just wanted to hang out and play in the pool, which is what we did, plus take naps. Everything worked out better when we didn't try to do everything and after resetting, we went back for a few more rides and the parade of lights.

Does your lifestyle work for you? Or against you, leaving you exhausted?

What changes would you like to make?

Life is what you make it.

Day 17 - Work Style

What is your work style? When do you work best?

Do you schedule the tough stuff when you are at your best? Do you do the easy stuff when you are at a lower energy level?

I've learned I do my best work from 7 am – 2 pm and then I need a break - to eat, exercise/do something physical, or walk around and talk to people. So, from 2 pm – 5 pm I do the easy stuff, like phone calls, filing, catch up, etc.

Scheduling work travel on the weekends or coaching calls on Monday or Fridays is a no no because I inevitably travel on those days, and I'd rather not reschedule client appointments. Overtime, I've learned when to keep my calendar clear to function better.

One of my clients, who is not a morning person, blocks off her calendar every day until 11 am so that she can take care of herself and send her children off to school at her pace and energy level before beginning work.

Do you take breaks when you get to a point where you are no longer productive?

Are you a morning person? Night owl? When are you at your best?

Does your work style match the requirements of the work you are doing or do you need to make adjustments?

We all have
the same 24 hours.

Day 18 - Family Time

Today's topic is family time and expectation setting.

I've seen a ton of posts about holiday time with family and they range from 'so happy to hang out with my family' to 'I'm dreading it, why do I do this to myself.'

Before getting divorced, I had been (unknowingly) isolated from my family. I'll never forget the weekend after I moved out when my brother and his girlfriend invited me to spend the day with them at the French Antique Market in Marin. I had the most marvelous day of fun and laughter. I hadn't realized how isolated I was and how much I missed hanging out with and being with my family.

Others don't want to spend time with family members because it is too negative or toxic, which means you may have to put a boundary in place to not put yourself in harm's way.

Do you want to live closer to family? Further away?

Do you have movie or game night, family reading time, or something fun for your family time?

What is your family time like? Does it nourish you or drain you?

Spend time with those you love.

Day 19 - Resetting

When do you feel like you need a mental health day or a reset?

When do you feel overwhelmed? What are the signs?

What are you doing (or can you do) to stay out of overwhelm?

I know there are several things that send me to the edge:
- Changes I don't have any control over
- A packed schedule with no choices (meaning I can't change or choose what to do or work on)
- Stuff I don't really want to do (I don't mean things like cleaning the house, I mean things that aren't in alignment with my goals, but I said yes to anyway)

Looking at this list control/freedom and alignment are important factors for me to lookout for.

I've put two solutions in place to help me stay on an even keel - I keep a day open after travel (meeting free) so I can catch up and follow up. I also stopped scheduling meetings on Mondays so that I can do the highest priority work at the beginning of the week.

What measures/changes can you put in place to prevent reaching the point of overwhelm or needing a mental health day?

Where's the
reset button?

Day 20 - Finances

What boundaries do you have in place regarding your finances?

During my divorce, I spent a few years with little income, a high level of debt, and uncertainty whether my one remaining credit card would work. It was stressful and not a time I care to repeat. Little by little I had to put boundaries in place to rebuild my finances and sense of security.

I know I have a high need for control over my finances to foster an acceptable level of psychological safety for myself. This also means I like to have a minimum amount in my bank account, so I don't have to worry when I make a purchase.

Student loans cause a lot of people a lot of stress. I don't like to have debt of any kind, so I set up my loan payments to include a little extra each month. It gave me peace of mind that I wouldn't be paying off those loans forever.

What measures do you have in place around money to foster good self-care?

Do you have any changes to make in this area?

Discover what works
best for you.

Day 21 - Week 3 Observations

This past week was about changes. Looking back, what observations do you have?

What changes did you make?

What has made a difference for you?

Sitting still, reflecting how how I was feeling led me to recognize what sends me into overwhelm and feeling like I can't do anything or nothing that I am doing is making a difference. Once I could see the triggers or signs, I could do something about it.

Before I learned to do that, I would just keep going, mistakenly believing I could work my way out of it. Thinking 'If I just did more' or 'I just need to finish this one last thing' led me to the 'heart attack' incident I shared earlier. Letting go of the belief that I had to do everything was a necessary change.

Do you need to make any additional changes around your self-care?

And if so, what changes would you like to make?

Positive thoughts only attract positive energy.

Day 22 - Self-care Toolbox

This week is about expanding our self-care toolbox. What's in your toolbox for self-care?

When I was sick and couldn't do anything but sit still for three days, I had plenty of time to contemplate my belly button, among other things...

We, the collective we, must figure out what works for us and what doesn't. Otherwise, we'll all end up in burnout land, unsatisfied, and unhappy. Or stuck there if we are already experiencing burnout.

One arrangement my husband and I implemented early on in our relationship is to try to cook together so no one person feels like they are doing everything. Same with cleaning. It's part of our 'marriage contract," my husband washes the dishes and I dry and put away.

He knows I hate washing dishes – they why behind it was a power struggle with my first live-in boyfriend where he had antiquated ideas of what roles women occupy. My husband doesn't like to do the dishes either, but he knows I hate it and why, so he washes them. I see this arrangement as one of my most essential self-care tools.

The most common self-care activities are sleep, listening to music, drinking water, relaxing, and going for a walk.

What self-care tools work best for you?

If you can't think of any, I've shared a few ideas on the Helpful Self-care Resources page before Day 15.

Self-care is
not one size fits all.

_____
_____
_____
_____
_____
_____
_____
_____
_____
_____
_____
_____
_____
_____
_____
_____
_____
_____

Day 23 - Priorities

What matters most to you - I mean this in a *priority* kind of way.

Do you require a few minutes of quiet time at the end of each workday before making dinner?

Do you require time outside each day? In the sunshine?

Do you have non-negotiables when it comes to your self-care?

Currently, my non-negotiables are sunshine, exercise, and time hanging out with my hubby. Moving to Washington State, with all its rain, I must go outside even if there isn't sun. And when the sun is out, I've been known to just stand in the doorway soaking it up.

Consequently, I bought a SAD lamp to use all winter. And now we plan time in January, February, and March somewhere sunny and, if possible, visiting family because hanging out with our aging parents is a priority for us.

What is a priority for you? What are your non-negotiables?

Control
the controllables.

Day 24 - Retooled Routines

If you retooled any of your routines around sleeping, exercise, food, meditation, etc....
- What changes did you make?
- How is it working?

Well, having been sick recently gave me a chance to rethink and redo a lot of things, especially around food and drink. I could hardly keep rice and sparkling water down. So that simplified a lot of things for me around food and eating.

A few months ago, I spoke with a friend lost 20 pounds eating a plant-based diet. Since learning more about her weight loss journey, I've spent a lot of time wondering what that would even look like for me. Having grown up on a farm with beef cattle and a side of beef in the freezer, I'm drawing a blank trying to imagine a plant-based diet for myself.

In rethinking my food habits, I realize I need to be more creative around food and reintroducing food slowly as I recover, which is the perfect opportunity to make some dietary changes.

What other changes would you like to make?

Does anyone
ever like change?

Day 25 - Saying No

NO is a complete sentence.

In 2011 when I took a job in San Francisco with an hour-long commute each way, I finally learned how to say no. I said no to everything that wasn't work, kid, or board related.

At first, it was hard for this inveterate people-pleaser to say no. It became easier over time when I realized the world wasn't going to end and people weren't going to hate me if I said no.

Now, I have no qualms about using the word no or saying no. I've given up saying "Yes" or "I'll think about it," when I mean no. It's been freeing.

Clarity gives us the strength to say no to nonessentials. This skill truly is a form of self-care and boundary setting.

Is the word no in your vocabulary?

Do you say yes when you mean no?

"Learn the slow 'yes' and the quick 'no.' " - Greg McKeown

Day 26 - Taking Risks

Are you playing it safe or are you taking calculated risks? Does this need to change?

Recently my husband and I joined the Vancouver Master Chorale. I hadn't sung in an organized choir since sixth grade, although I had taken singing lessons in 2004 when I joined a community theater group.

Just the thought of having to memorize words/lyrics terrified me to the point where I almost didn't audition. Thankfully, I learned that the choir performs using musical scores. In our first performance we sang Faure's Requiem which I hadn't played (usually I play trombone) or sung before.

Timing-wise, we were part of a group from our Chorale which joined other choirs to perform the same music at Carnegie Hall. The entire experience was fantastic – even the 4-hour rehearsals. The sound inside Carnegie Hall was amazing and we had a marvelous and unforgettable concert.

If we hadn't taken a chance and auditioned for the Chorale when we did, we would have missed the opportunity to perform at Carnegie Hall.

Where are you going outside your comfort zone and taking a risk?

Change happens outside your comfort zone.

Day 27 - Support System

Today's topic is your support system.

What support system(s) do you have in place?

Friends, family?
Groups? Colleagues?

Overtime, I have cultivated a trusted set of friends and family and I feel like it is a good support system. Same with the groups and organizations I spend time with. Meanwhile, I've tried to distance myself from negativity and naysayers and minimize time spent with them.

Relying on yourself 100% of the time is exhausting.

What type of support systems do you have in place?

Do you need more support?

Is there anything you can outsource?

If you need to build your support team, which friends, family, professionals, or others do you want on your team?

We go further together
than alone.

Day 28 - Week 4 Observations

What observations do you have from this past week of examining what's in your self-care toolbox? What, if any, mindset shifts did you experience?

Well, I noticed my biggest mindset shift was making the best of things when things did not go as planned. In a word, resilience.

When my mom came to visit for the first time since we moved to Washington, I came down with Covid and had to isolate most of her visit.

All the fun activities I had planned didn't happen. Instead, my mom hung out with my husband and boys (who were not the best tour guides), while I hung out by myself with ample time to sit and think.

Also, since I couldn't eat, I had plenty of time to rethink my diet and exercise routines – both of which require rethinking and implementing changes.

What is going well for your self-care? What isn't?

What tools/techniques are you using?

Did you discover any new ones?

Choose the right tool
for the job.

Day 29 - Takeaways

What observations or takeaways do you have after paying closer attention to your self-care?

Did you mix things up or try anything new these last 28 days?

For me, I noticed it's the small things. Usually I brush my teeth, go to the bathroom, and then fall into bed to read a few pages before falling asleep. After hosting a self-care webinar, I took the suggestion of one of the panelists and implemented a new nighttime routine to take better care of my skin.

I placed my face cleanser and moisturizer in the same location as my toothbrush. Even with this minor change, I find that sometimes I wash my face and moisturize it well, and other times I go to bed with makeup on.

While it's more of a regular thing now, it's not an 'every night routine' and I figure 2-3 days a week is better than none!

What are you doing to mix things up?!? What have the results been?

What are your takeaways from your focus on self-care?

It's never too late to make a change.

Day 30 - Celebrate

Take a moment to notice and celebrate all you've done for yourself over the last 30 days. It may be helpful to look back at your notes and then write about the progress you have made.

It's the acknowledgement and act of celebrating that cements in our brains the good habits, experiences and outcomes.

Overall, my thought is that I eat well and I need to eat less sugar, less alcohol, and more plant based/centric meals. Generally, I feel good and healthy, a week of Covid notwithstanding, and I could use more movement/more intense exercise.

Exploring boot camp and yoga options along with strength training is next up for me – I need to exercise more intensely and more consistently for my overall health.

What changes have become habits for you, if any? What changes do you want to make going forward?

How will you celebrate the changes you've made for yourself?

Celebrate your accomplishments!

What self-care activities work best for you?

Take a walk

Meditate

Write in my journal

Take a nap

Hang out with my pet

Binge-watch a show

Meet a friend

Exercise

Time outside

Cooking

Sending birthday cards

Quiet time

Gardening

Go for a run

Singing

Playing videogames

Hang out with my partner

Read a book

Coloring

Playing a Game

Pulling a Tarot Card

Watch a funny video

Hiking

Trying a new recipe

Talk to my mom

Writing a note to a friend

Taking vitamins

Sitting in the sun

Favorite sport

Playing an instrument

Dancing

Write in Your Favorites

In Gratitude

I'd specifically like to acknowledge intuitive business coach, Elysia Skye. When we met in 2018 who knew how different and amazing our lives would be now. Thank you for your wisdom, mindfulness advice, and your inspiration to change up my nighttime routine!

www.thebrilliancemethod.com

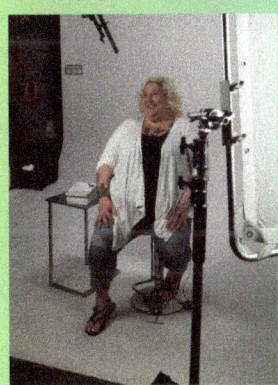

Also integral to bringing this workbook to fruition (as well as my book What's Next for My Career? and my other workbooks) is Megs Thompson. Your brilliance, sense of humor and writing and publishing skills made this process a breeze. Thank you for your expertise!

www.megswrites.com

Thank you to everyone who participated with me in the self-care challenges in 2018 and 2022, it was eye-opening each time. I learned more about myself and implemented important changes, some of which are detailed here.

Final Thoughts

I hope you have been able to use this 30 Days for Better Self-care workbook as a guide to help you understand your needs better and learn how to best care for yourself. My wish for you is that you have found the help you need to put better self-care practices in place for yourself. It's easier to thrive when you are not overwhelmed or too busy taking care of others to take care of yourself.

"The moment you connected with me was transformative. Right before that I felt so confused and overwhelmed. You saw me and pointed me in the right direction. You had my back every step on the way. You have a magical way of seeing what someone needs and proving that in a quiet and gentle way. Thank you!"

Tara G. – Attorney, Widow & Mom of 5

"Thanks to Sonya for helping me prepare for and advance in the selection process for the role I begin today. Even if it hadn't worked out, our conversations helped me develop a fuller appreciation for my experience and the potential of my next steps."

John L. - Attorney & Single dad of 2

"Sonya is amazing because she is creative and intellectual. She's patient (thank goodness) and uses her intuition to guide me in a way that I'm comfortable with. I really appreciate that! I am so fortunate to have received her guidance in starting my business (and the work continues). Thank you, Sonya!"

Entrepreneur Elysia S.

I look forward to learning more about you and your self-care journey. If you find you need additional help, please get in touch and we can brainstorm which changes will be the most helpful for you.

Schedule a Call

Check out my other books, workbooks, and audiobooks on Amazon.